New Covenant Bound

D0916632

KENTUCKY VOICES

New Covenant Bound

T. Crunk

THE UNIVERSITY PRESS OF KENTUCKY

Scholarly publisher for the Commonwealth,
serving Bellarmine University, Berea College, Centre College of Kentucky,
Eastern Kentucky University, The Filson Historical Society, Georgetown
College, Kentucky Historical Society, Kentucky State University,
Morehead State University, Murray State University, Northern Kentucky
University, Transylvania University, University of Kentucky, University of
Louisville, and Western Kentucky University.
All rights reserved.

Editorial and Sales Offices: The University Press of Kentucky
663 South Limestone Street, Lexington, Kentucky 40508-4008
www.kentuckypress.com

Though based on actual persons and events, the persons and events
depicted here are fictional. A number of place names have also been
changed.

14 13 12 11 10   5 4 3 2 1

Library of Congress Cataloging-in-Publication Data

Crunk, Tony.
  New covenant bound / T. Crunk.
     p. cm. — (Kentucky voices)
  Includes index.
  ISBN 978-0-8131-2599-2 (pbk. : alk. paper)
  1. Kentucky—Poetry. 2. Land Between the Lakes (Ky. and Tenn.)—
Poetry. I. Title.
  PS3553.R7855N48 2010
  811'.54—dc22   2010017512

Manufactured in the United States of America.

 Member of the Association of
American University Presses

To Maria, from the beginning.

To Tracy Jordan, David Nickell, Della Oliver, Margaret Chambers, Ray and Shara Parish, Chris Wallace, Paul Yambert, Jim Atchison, Kenny Fralicx, Phil and Georgia Harrell, and the many other people of Between the Rivers who shared their lives and stories with such kindness, and without whose generosity this book would not have been possible. It is offered with deepest gratitude, in honor of your profound love for this sacred place.

Contents

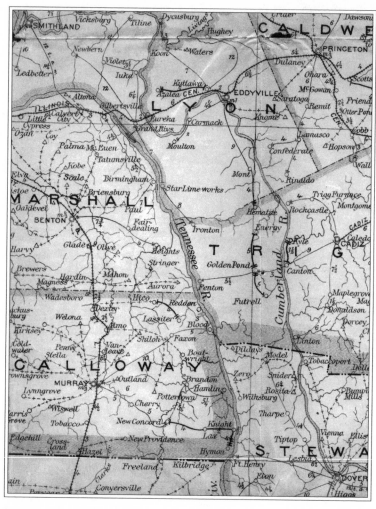

Between the Rivers, 1907

Memoriam

Between 1935 and 1938, some 110 families in western Kentucky were moved from their homes between the Tennessee and Cumberland Rivers to make way for the Federal Resettlement Administration's Kentucky Woodlands National Wildlife Refuge.

Between 1936 and 1944, some 2,400 families in western Kentucky and Tennessee were moved from their homes along the Tennessee River to make way for the Tennessee Valley Authority's Kentucky Lake.

Between 1958 and 1963, some 1,400 families in western Kentucky and Tennessee were moved from their homes along the Cumberland River to make way for the Army Corps of Engineers' Lake Barkley.

Between 1963 and 1969, some 980 families in western Kentucky and Tennessee were moved from their homes in the area between the two lakes to make way for the Tennessee Valley Authority's Land Between the Lakes National Recreation Area.

Though no official count exists, it is estimated that between 28,000 and 30,000 people were forcibly removed from their homes, many of them multiple times, to make way for these federal land- and water-management projects.

*   *   *

For Birmingham, Kentucky, evacuated and demolished, 1937: "Birmingham folk have ever been a home loving people, the children and grandchildren of the early settlers now occupying the first old home sites. . . . Birmingham still clings to her beloved traditions — her citizens get great pleasure living in the past — a restful place it has proven to be in a rapidly changing world."

—Leon Freeman and Edward Olds,
The History of Marshall County, Kentucky (1933)

I. Summons

Your words will issue from the earth; your voice
will come like a ghost's from the ground.
— Isaiah 29:4

The only ones that liked it were the ones that got something out of it. And the only ones that got something out of it were the ones that already had something.

Needless to say, your grandfather and I were amongst the ones that didn't like it.

Nightfall

Blue clouds
smother a pale ghostmoon
above the cluster of roofs
like hulls
of capsized boats.

Peach trees in the yard
go on with their dumb show
locusts' tiny engines
whirring, may-moths
tittling the window screen
of my father's kitchen.

Lamp on the table
remains unlit
letting darkness take it — day gone
beyond all ease.

In the next room
my grandmother,
watching night take the houses
and the street
watching it take her hand
resting on the sill,
is five years old
sitting on her iron bedstead
at the window
looking downriver.

For her
the streetlamp at the corner
flickering on
is the spotlight

of a freight packet
rounding Haddock's Elbow
searching for the Birmingham landing . . .

A thousand miles away
a thousand miles from home
I'm watching
the same white moon
come clear

weary rounder
casting its blind eye
over the tar-shingled sheds
along the alley
the blue shirts
hanging on a line

and in through the open
window where I sit
wondering how
it could all come down
to this — a handful
of change on the dresser
a pocketknife

my empty coat
exhausted on a chair
my father's face in the mirror
the light around him now
all falling
and fallen.

We started out seeing the government cars parked along a road or by a creek or off in a pasture. Started seeing the men with their maps and their spyglasses and measuring rods out walking the riverbank.

Your grandfather came across a couple of them out back of the cane field.

There'd been talk of a dam for years. People figured they were finally getting around to building one. But we all figured it was going to be just a little spill dam with a navigation lock. Like the one down at Dover.

Then the papers started talking about an electric plant. And a lake. Said they were already building several down in Tennessee.

The papers would say one thing one week and something else the next. People were let to believe pretty much what they wanted.

Then finally it started to come clear. And then they called the big meeting to tell us all. Officially.

We were to be moved off the land and the land flooded.

Parting

Father —
there is no departing
only worlds
passing through our hands.

There is no arriving
only days of rest
or of return.
When I came to tell you

I was leaving New Covenant
moving from Kentucky
you were planting roses
along the alley fence

where no amount of bonemeal
or kneeling
your hands working the dirt
could make them grow

rooted in the coal chips
and cinders
though every several years
you tried again.

I knelt beside you
held the canes
as you sifted peat into the holes
packed the roots

saying nothing
sunset lowering its orange sails
twilight's thin veil
darkening.

Finally: "Son
is there any future
in what you are doing?"

Father — still
so many years beyond
I have no answer for you
only this:

the future was
a house you lived in
that could not stand.
The future

was a mirror
where I saw my face
sinking slowly into nothing.
The future is this

shard of blue willow plate
remnant of time's
borrowed scrip
now staining my pocket.

There's two ways to ring a church bell. One way, you pull the rope and let go, so the two claps come one right after the other. That's the way they ring it for church service or a camp meeting. They call that the meeting bell.

The other way, you pull the rope and hold it, then let go, so there's a little wait between the first clap and the second. And when you hear that, you drop what you're doing and come running, because that's the way they ring it when there's a fire or an accident, or someone has taken sick or has died. It means someone is in need of help. And they call that the mourning bell.

They called the big meeting at the Bethel Church to tell people what they were going to do about building this dam. Me and your grandfather were there, along with everybody else from that end of the county. Trucks and wagons were pulled in everywhere, all around the churchyard, all up and down the road.

Before it started, you'd have thought it was a Fourth of July picnic. People gathered around in little groups, visiting and laughing and talking. Children running and shouting everywhere.

They all thought they had something to celebrate. Thought they were going to get rich off this dam project. Thought that if they *had* to sell their land, they'd just hold the government to whatever price *they* wanted.

There were three TVA men there. When it came time to start, they asked the preacher to go inside and ring the church bell to call the meeting to order. The preacher had already spent that morning with them, showing them around the countryside. He knew what was about to be said that afternoon.

He went into the church vestibule, and he rung the bell, all right.

We all heard the first clap, but then there was that little wait before we heard the second clap. And right away it struck people, clear as a gunshot.

He rung the bell that way three times.

By the third time, there was hardly a word being said by anybody. And there wasn't a soul laughing anymore.

Those three TVA men were city people. They had no idea what they'd just heard.

But everybody else knew. And they were all gathered up close around the churchhouse steps, looking at those men, listening and waiting, solemn as a funeral.

Leaving New Covenant

1. Waiting for the 12:16

Midnight ticked away
on time
station to station
around the clock

sleepwalkers
scattered along the benches
resting
beneath their burdens

the last light gone out
in the New Central
Hotel across the street
rows of black windows
now dark as heaven's caves.

Phone poles along the tracks
marched off into the night
only their shadows
for coats

the moon
rusting in its socket

and we who inherit the earth —
that snow
will yet cover us
with its little
hieroglyphic tokens
of the life to come.

2. Landscape: Muhlenberg County

A house
leaning into the earth
seeking its level

smoke at the chimney
lingering
like prayer.

Beyond
along a ridge
pines gathering snow
white scrip
in their thin arms

saving against the day of rest
that never comes —
only tomorrow
and tomorrow.

Cold
numbing the air
honing the tears
of the bluecane
into thorns.

3. Burning Ground

Black water of the Ohio
slid by in creases thick with December

the train pulled up along a siding
to let another through

waking me. On the opposite shore
the refineries

like towers of besieged cities
blazing latticework of red and yellow lights

gray steam and smoke
shadows of men passing through them

and sixty feet in the air in the clear night
a blue hand of flame

pulsing above a gas jet.
The dream I woke from: a spider

paying out its web
bone by flawless bone — frail skeleton

of light, tiny ladder of mercy
raised up on the burning ground.

They came through with their spyglasses and their measuring rods and marked it off all up and down the cove. On rocks and trees. On barns and corncribs.

Three hundred and eighty-seven. Three hundred and eighty-seven.

They wouldn't paint it on your house. And they wouldn't paint it on any church buildings. They'd set a post in the yard with a marker on it instead. But other than that, it didn't matter. Three hundred and eighty-seven, whitewashed on everything.

That's how high the flood level was to reach. Three hundred and eighty-seven feet.

We sat in the yard all afternoon and watched them the day they worked their way across Hebron Ridge back of the house.

First it was Callum's Woods. They whitewashed a big *three* on one tree trunk, then a big *eight* on another one, then a big *seven* on another.

Then they worked their way down and whitewashed it at the foot of the bluff behind the spring. Then they three-hundred-and-eighty-sevened Lenox Furniss's barn, then my brother Buell's smithing shed. Around sunset we watched them sink one of those marker posts next to Aunt Molly Burke's sitting porch.

Hadn't anybody told us yet. Officially. But it didn't take any measuring rod to see that all those numbers were being whitewashed above the level of our house.

Two more years and everything we had in this world would be under a hundred foot of water.

Self : Portrait

Under rivers of darkness
I am walking
the city a cathedralled cave of light
I have come to
as shadows must
to survive.

Walls in the wind
a jukebox moon
I cross South Union Bridge
counting the signs I have chosen.

One: a man made of lightning
striding across a billboard —
At Your Service * * * *
* * * * *Reddy Kilowatt.*

Two: at Third and Broad
a blind
street preacher singing
"Wonder is my mother
on that train
on that train . . ."

Wandering the dead
of night
I come to the end
of my palindrome
turn back
with the day's conclusions:

A circle
is defined by
distance from a center.

The wheel is nothing
splayed ring of ribs
without the stake
through its heart
to turn on.

Behind St. Jude's
raw smoke
rises from a rusting oil barrel
enters the sky
where tomorrow
will begin again at zero.

I wait for the light
at Lexington and Main.

Three:
a stringless mandolin
hanging
in a pawnshop window

tiny ladder
rising
now from a heart.

Brother Hecht, over at Muddy Fork, preached a whole revival about it that fall.

Said that it would never come to pass.

Said the Lord had made a covenant with Noah in the ninth chapter of Genesis that the earth would never again be destroyed by water.

Said that if it did come to pass, it wouldn't be the work of the Lord, but of man. Or worse.

Said the governments of men had best be careful transgressing the covenant of the Lord.

Traveler's Rest

Once I lay awake
in a cinderblock room

leafing through the Gideons'
my fingers

five white stems
that would never bloom

following
words along a page —

> " . . . across a harrowed field
> the wind raised up a man of red dust
>
> to send into the world
> blood of the land in his veins
>
> salt of the earth for flesh
> sorrows of the unremembered
>
> on his tongue.
> But how shall the dust then speak
>
> knowing itself to be but dust?
> And how shall the dust set forth
>
> knowing it will only return
> to dust?"

Father —
in my dream that night

you came to me
stood by the alley gate

calling

offering to take back
your old coats.

II. Bethel Grove

Oh where are our dear fathers?
Oh where are our dear fathers?
They are down in the valley praying.
Day is breaking in my soul.
      — "Bright Morning Stars,"
                hymn, traditional

Return

1.

Back through the trackless
        dust and testaments
back through
        the blind names and photographs
I cross
        Green River by twilight
pulling the eastern
        darkness behind me
into the rising west Kentucky night
        its power to heal
its power to bring down
        and make nothing

back through the bus trips
        and found coins and baptisms
through the crippled hours
        and landmarks
dropping down the Knobs
        into Muhlenberg
night moths
        flashing in the headlights
sparks
        released from their flame
off to the left
        and to the right
pools of white spotlight
        nailing the black
stripped landscape —
        shovels
squatting in the coal fields
        scraping away

the overburden
          raising the dark waste to the surface
smell of sulfur
          smoke and dust

back through the links of chain
          and fallen ashes
back through the grace notes
          and little offerings
crossing the Purchase farmlands
          where the rich hand of blessing
has passed over
          and moved on
planks of the barns and cattlesheds
          like ribs
separating
          breath of life gone out of them
burley stalks
          unclenching
corn in its tattered silks
          whispering

back through the scattered bricks
          and lost mirrors
back to the western lakes
          where Bethel Grove
lies buried beneath the black water
          of my grandmother's memory
crossing the Barrens
          by a hardscrabble moon
gospel fighting static
          out of Thornton Gap:
"The Father
          waits over the way
in a land
          that is fairer than day

to prepare us
           our mansion of rest . . ."

I am going back
           to seek my place
in the abandoned past
           running
shoulder to shoulder
           with the Illinois Central
long iron rail
           by short cross tie
endless ladder
           pointing home.

2.

Dawn hauls in
           with the coal trucks
grinding down
           the causeway to Gracey Landing
to unload.
           First light:
leaning on a rail
           looking south
from the dam's observation deck
           — penstock and tailrace
pumping the dark heart
           buried deep below me —
watching the lake
           give up its ghosts
white mist
           retreating back into the coves
and locust hollows
           back up Dividing Ridge
where the elders
           and elms and sycamores gather.

22

Sunk beneath the spread waters
        the river itself
lost to the land
        channel buoys marking the grave
link chain of barges
        fishing boats and runabouts
already drawing
        long scars across the surface

lake gulls
        working the shallows —
confettied scraps
        of gray light
banking and falling
        falling
pulling free
        to rise again.

They were married on one of the old steam packets, on their wedding trip up to Cerulean Springs.

"Took cabin fare, too," Grandpa Woodford said. "Wouldn't take deck fare on such a trip as that."

They would've been your great-great-grandparents, Grandma and Grandpa Woodford.

He was a tobacco buyer out of Clarksville, Tennessee. She was from over east, in Trigg County. They'd met at a school fair in Birmingham.

He told her that if she'd let him court her, he'd take her to Cerulean Springs for a honeymoon.

"So she did," he said, "and I did."

You've seen the pictures. Them sitting on that long porch of the Springs Hotel, in their summer shirts. Drinking mint tea out of crystal goblets.

They named Mother after the boat they were married on — *The Sallie Grace.*

Sunday Outings

Beyond backwash and slackwater
      west out of Union Hill
driving the old ferry road
      creek willows sheltering the Cumberland
calm here
      in its broad bed below the dam
all sinking away behind
      with late summer's dry dust
as I make for the Dover Trail
      a bank of low hills
folding down into turkey meadows
      and spring rills
Holly Cove to Fairdealing
      where I branch off on the hard road
the Trail
      drawing me down
a quarter mile of maplewood
      spread south to the lakes
thin shawl of white clouds
      feathering off
blue morning
      opening its hand to me —
places I could never find again
      roads I could never retrace . . .

             *   *   *

We walked
the broken trail
of the logging road

reclaimed by
burdock and blackthorn
coming to a stand

25

of river birch
hard by the shore
my father

moving down the bank
to cast a few
my brother and I

not fishing yet
scratching around
instead

in the shallow pit
grown over
with poke and ironweed

pulling vines away
to look
for foundation stones

racing
to stand together on
the mossed over

brick steps
leading
down into the water . . .

           *   *   *

A hewn log
saddle back cabin

a woman in dark homespun
a kettle

boiling in the woodyard
smoke of her fire

sifting up into the noonlight.
Behind her

an empty tobacco barn
a mule

penned in the shade.
Before her

a man with a camera
lining them up

with the sign
that says —

Homestead
1870

An Exhibit of
Living History . . .

                      *   *   **

Snow's thin hands
sift down
among the ancient hickories

and broken headstones
filling in
the beveled Chinese inscriptions —
laborers

brought here in the 1850s
to work the iron furnace
at Little Cypress.

Spirits
cannot cross water

so they wander and return
to a foreign land
no home in this world

or the next.
A breeze lifts
and we hear them —
a few locust pods

dried hard to their branches
clacking dully together
— shards of temple bells.

Grandma Woodford said, "I guess anything would seem like a letdown after a wedding trip to Cerulean Springs. But I had no idea Mr. Woodford had bought the sorriest piece of land between the rivers to move us on and try to farm."

They couldn't afford much. Couldn't afford bottom land.

Parts of the home place were so steep you could just about stand it on edge and plow both sides. Parts were just scalds and gullies, even back then, where they'd dug out the hematite banks long years before. Back when the iron bloomeries were still running.

But they managed to somehow squeeze a living out of it. And Mother and Papa squeezed a living out of it.

And me and your grandfather were doing our best with it before we lost it. Though by then, a little corn and sorghum cane was about all it would give us.

But that was a good, strong house Grandpa Woodford built. Good enough to raise three generations in. And start on a fourth.

Your father was the last child born in that house.

Elders

High fanlight of late morning
        whitens the road
threading the twin lakes south
        Tan Lick to Dewport
now dipping to cross Greves's Run
        two shitepoke
green ascetics
        standing on one leg
in the gravel shallows
        the Trail now rising
steep to the cut
        scored along Pease Bluff
fingers of water
        streaking the limestone face
scrub pines at the margins
        drawing
their noonhour shadows
        back into themselves.
Pulling off
        on a narrow turnout
overlooking
        a scarp of red cedars
I see across
        on the other side
a loose cluster of buildings
        near a boat ramp
I know would be Cordyn
        and I know that Bethel Grove
would lie
        another mile to the south
there
        where I can just make out

a white sail gliding
          among the arrowpoints
of light
          barbing the water . . .

                    *   *   *

My father remembers
fire: blown sparks
from his Uncle Buell's smithing iron
scorching red
eyes in the lilac leaves,
transparent scarves of yellow flame
smoking up from the locust boles
into a lowering February
sky — him and his father

burning off a new tobacco bed,
him and his grandfather hunting
camped on a bluff above the Cumberland
the two of them
sitting under scattershot stars
his grandfather telling him
of seeing
as a boy

The General Clifton
blow its boiler
off the Birmingham landing,
my father dreaming
that night
of hearing the stricken
cries of the perishing
of seeing that fire
out on the water . . .

                    *   *   *

My father remembers
a needlepoint picture:
Jesus seated in Glory
with the words

Christ is the Head
        Of This House
The Unseen Guest
        At Every Meal
The Silent Listener
        To Every Conversation

that hung above his father's
kitchen chair
who'd lean back after Sunday dinner
and sing out

"Well I'm most done traveling
this rough rocky road
and it's time my soul headed home" —
a game he had with the kids

— who'd sing out
"Papa
what will you do
if you can't afford the hearse?"

"Sit on my bed
and wait for angels to come."

"What will you do
if you can't afford the preacher?"

"Pay him with quarters
I stole from the moon."

"Papa
what will you do
if you can't afford the casket?"

"Charge it to the wind"
he'd sing
"and let the dust settle it . . ."

                    *   *   *

My father remembers lying awake
listening to the locusts in the orchard

chirring to split their skins
listening for the screech owl

haunting the cedars' attic rooms
and finally *The Jackson Flyer*

blue traveler
taking the high curve out of Orton Station

unwinding her long black veil across the Barrens
moaning it out by midnight —

once for those she takes away
twice for those she's leaving.

Sometimes, even now, after forty-odd years, the sun will play tricks with my eyes.

I'll look out the kitchen door here and think I see my trellis full of yellow roses. See the bee martins flitting in and out amongst them.

I'll see the wild cherries and hickories, the orchard beyond the yard. The blackberry thickets all down the bank to the creek, where the peppermint started.

Come spring, the daylilies by the front steps were the first thing to bloom. Them, and the apple rose by the cellar door.

When it got warm enough to unshutter the windows, I'd have the boys go down and gather some of that sweet river clay, and I'd rub down the fire box and the hearth bricks with it. I'd clip a vine of flowering blue-monk and twine it around the grate.

The house would fill up with a warm breeze coming up off the river, and it felt like being borned again.

I think it's my roses I miss the most. We never could get them to grow proper here in town.

Homecoming

Gaither to Mt. Oak
　　　the Trail winds down
the long mid-afternoon
　　　hour of jarfly and grasshopper
hour of dirtdauber and yellowjacket
　　　opens out to a broad hollow
flat of loose rock and stickerweed
　　　scar of an unnamed
crossroad settlement
　　　dismantled
and given over
　　　to Park land
a few paths
　　　bleeding off the main road
burrowing into sawbrier
　　　and jackberry thickets
a few clearings among the trees
　　　old homesites
given over to broomsage and sumac
　　　love vine and chicory.
In one
　　　a crutch of broken fence
separating nothing
　　　wind from wind
the bluecane entwining it.
　　　In one
goldfinches glinting
　　　like a handful of coins
scattered
　　　and rescattered
among the thistle.
　　　Above another

a flock of starlings licking out
       retreating
tongue of black flame
       across a pale white sky . . .

                *   *   *

Two things of my grandmother's
I was allowed to look at:
her Bible with the hand-tinted illustrations,
Jacob's Ladder The Camp at Canaan
The Master Calms the Storm,
with the marriages and deaths

the births and numbers of the years
in spider script across the front pages
I'd trace with my fingers
my own name and year of my birth
the last of the list
facing a blank page.

The other: her hatbox of old photographs
she kept beneath her bed,
portraits in rusting sepia
snapshots cracking and taped over
names of lost friends lost relations
penciled on the backs.

I came to picture hell
as a place in the Bible illustrations
like the Hebrew children
standing in the fiery furnace
or the people going down in the water
begging to be let on the ark.

I came to picture heaven
as the place in the photographs
Bethel Grove

came to picture us at death
gathered at the river
waiting for the ferry boat

that would take us over
pictured somewhere on the other side
a white house
white curtains at the open windows
morning breeze
leafing through the redbuds

the grape arbor and cornflowers
by the garden fence
and beneath the ancient poplar
a table spread
our elders
in gaunt coats and Sunday dresses

graceful and unburdened now
coming and going in the light
about the house and yard
preparing the homecoming.
I picture them stopping
to listen

as the bell at the ferry landing
tolls our arrival
picture our mothers and our fathers
coming down to the front gate
stepping out into the dust
of the road to watch for us.

Some people saved up their Briar Rose flour sacks. They came printed with a gingham pattern on the inside. You could wash them and iron them out flat and put them up, and if you had enough, you could have a whole gingham print wall.

Usually, we just used newspapers, though we had to change them more often. Then you cut pictures out of the slick papers, the catalogues and magazines, to put over top of the newspaper.

We all got to pick out the pictures we wanted to put up. Mother put pictures of furniture over her chair and over the sink. Papa would pick the biggest picture of an automobile he could find for over his chair. Then he'd put smaller pictures of tools or new farm machines around it.

Buell picked pictures of cars, too, and pictures of cities, big buildings and churches, all lit up at night.

Inez and I didn't care what the pictures were. We just tried to save enough of the slick papers to cover the wall up over our bed. We liked to lie awake at night and watch the firelight dancing on all the colors.

Mother would save little verses from the newspapers and put them up on the wall by the table. Papa would read them to us during meals, or afterward. Before it was time to change the paper again, we would all learn the new verses by heart.

I still remember a good many of them —

> "Beneath the oak leaves murm'ring lowly
> Whispering to themselves apart
> Of a dark train moving slowly
> Sleeps the angel of my heart . . ."

The last time I talked with Papa where he could understand me, about two days before he died, we were talking about that.

He said, "Do you still remember the one about the sweet rose of heaven?"

And I said, "Yes, Papa. I remember that one."

And he said, "How did that one go?"

I think he knew it himself, still. But it was one of his favorites, and he liked to hear me tell it. So I told it to him.

I still remember it, too. And this is some forty-odd years later.

Remembrance

After the last leg
      Jons Creek to Titus
circling back east on the main highway
      dodging the logging trucks
the tourists and travel trailers
      wayfarers all
seeking an evening's home
      away from home
after finding the gravel turnoff
      past the wrought iron
gates of Newly Cemetery
      just shy of Clark Ferry Bridge
looking for the one place
      I still know well
a rutted path along a low creek
      back into the sheltering
cool of a woods
      and out again into the clearing
where Dothan Pond
      gathers late sunlight
clouds' lost dominion
      in white ruins
passing weightlessly over
      I leave the car
make my way down
      the muddy flat of the creekbank
kneel where the water
      folds its smooth sleeve
gently around a maple root
      a racer snake
slicking off
      like a signature into the weeds.

I sift a few white stones
     ungathered grains of time
through my fingers
     brush away
a bit of husk remaining
     and I'm remembering
too
     Grandmother —

       "Sweet rose of heaven
       You seem forever
       Blushing in the noon-day sun
       To delight us every one.

       "And may you sweetly
       Fill life completely
       With your fragrance and your love
       Of your home in heaven above . . ."

III. The Crossing

The land goes down in ruin. . . .
Every town is forsaken. No one dwells there.
— Jeremiah 4:20, 29

Signs

Late rain
rolls up over Hebron Ridge

stitching the earth
with its news of the everlasting

moves north up the valley
and out across Carr's Bluff

trailing its garments
toward the Barrens

white mist
like winding sheets

shreds across the eldercanes
and thorntrees

last hour of day
clearing now to the west

offering
what signs it can:

clouds bearing horses
clouds bearing fire.

The winter Papa died was one of the hardest people could remember. Snow stayed knee-deep all of January. The ice broke one of the big sycamores out back of the yard.

Mother said it wasn't so, but I still believe it was the thought of leaving the home place that killed him.

They couldn't get through to Birmingham to buy him a casket, so we had Ike Johns make him one. Mother lined it on the inside with white linen. Aunt Beck made him a red satin pillow.

They had to carry him by sled to Colton Cemetery. Some of the men stayed up all night the night before, keeping a fire to thaw the ground. They dug out as much of a grave as they could and had to chop the rest out with axes.

Somebody said later — and it was a bitter thing, but true — what a shame it was to have to work so hard to bury him, when they would just have to dig him up again that spring.

That was when the TVA came to move all the graveyards.

Making Camp

Crickets
stuttering among the pond reeds

once blessing the harvest day
now trying to call back

the conjure words.
White dove

once at a window
now grieving pine to pine.

Gray thin of moon
fading in

deepening dusk blue —
the light they say the dead

see by.
I raise my tent

beside the still water
make a bed of rusted needles

gather black bones of wood
for fire, wondering

which of these is the token
that will gain me passage

which the little offering
that will release me.

In one of the graves at Woodson Chapel, they found a pearl-handled dagger.

In one of the graves in St. Stephens, they found a bag of gold coins. Somebody said they were Spanish.

One of the graves at Bethlehem Church had already been emptied. There was nothing in it.

In Nickell, they found two brothers buried in cast iron coffins, each with a little window at the face.

They'd laid out a new cemetery in New Covenant, and that's where most were taken. We had no idea where we were going to end up, so that's where we had them move Papa, along with the rest of the family. Looking back now, it seems like a sign.

If the family had somewhere else they wanted one buried, the TVA would try to do it for them, up to twenty miles away. If they couldn't find any family to speak for one, they just left that one there.

So in the end, they gathered some together, and scattered others here and yon, and left a few behind.

I do believe that when the good Lord comes to raise the dead, he'll do a somewhat better job of it.

Twilight

Father — I see you in last light
your black coat

crossing the clearing to the far birchwood
late breeze feathering your white hair

your lantern your beggar's cup of sight
disappearing

as you enter the darkness at the edge of the trees
and I am left

your son a stranger to you now
your shadow bound for wandering the earth.

And death is this thread of spider's web snapping.

Dragonflies setting off across Dothan Pond
bear the soul away

to the pastures of plenty
where angels sit in the branches of the sugartrees

whispering, wings held close to their bodies
and it is always twilight.

Clean as a cane cutting . . . and awful to see.

All the timber below the flood level had to be cut. If you had a way to haul it off, they'd let you sell it. If you didn't, they'd come through after you were gone and cut it and burn it.

Everywhere you went that last year, the woods were coming down. Clean as a cane cutting.

It sent the wild game roaming in droves, all uprooted and half-crazy. We had a fox come running in our kitchen door one evening. Had a brood of wild turkeys set up underneath the smokehouse. It was just unheard of.

Of course, the houses had to come down, too. They would move your house for you, but you had to have someplace to move it to. If you didn't, it was just too bad. After you moved out, they would send in a crew of men to knock it down and burn it, too.

Toward the end, there was a number of times they burned a house before the people were moved out. Some of the last ones to hold on lost everything they owned that way. Shameful, just shameful, to think anybody could be treated such as that.

At first, though, people would gather to watch. I think they just couldn't believe it was really going to happen. We went over to watch them take down the old Spiceman home, and the Darnells' place.

But then it just got to be too pitiful. And people could see it was true. So they stopped going to watch.

Eden

1.

Window
lying in the thistle
eye that never closed

burnt chimney
rising above the goldenrod
like Christ blessing the children

iron hinge
in the ashes
wings that fell to earth

broken teeth of the cemetery fence
a sacred harp
rusting

shadows
of the mournful cypress
— house you were born in.

2.

The sky gives up now
goes dark

willows
in their poorcoats

keen quietly by the stream
the maples

homeless
their kingdom of leaves

fallen in ruin
three crows

black prophets
lift up from the dirt road ahead

black pods of the catalpa
hanging

like our other lives
— stillborn.

Our only sin was being born where we were. And not giving up on a land that often spited us.

Our only sin was not having what they thought was enough. And being forced to take what they called help.

Exile

Sunset's coat of many colors
fades out over Hebron Ridge

line of electric pylons
great scarecrows

marching south out of Gilbertsville
down into Harmony and Stowe and into Tennessee.

Smoke from the fire I've built
rises like my shadow,

released, casting its body below.
And all I can see before me

is the thin web of lines in my hand
and my hand —

Hope Everlasting etched in my left
Loss Evermore in my right.

Night is the quiet closing of the two together
like tired wings

as we learn to pray
the prayer of our fathers:

O give light
give light

or take back the darkness

for thine is the kingdom
and the power

but ours is the line of torches
moving slowly down to the river.

We were amongst the last to leave. We hadn't meant to be. But they had found no place to move us to.

The crossing was at Oldham Ferry. Not but two miles, but it was the longest trip I ever took. Everything we owned in the world tied up on the back of a truck.

The countryside looked like the day after Judgment. Houses gone, burnt down to ashes. The ones still standing, dark and hollow as a skull bone.

Graves in the churchyard were yawning open and left empty. The woods looked like a stubblefield, timber piled for burning. Fields unplowed and unplanted, just raw places on the land.

We made the landing by late afternoon.

The last we saw of home was off the back of that ferryboat, the sun going down red over Hebron Ridge, us straining to make out Bethel Grove one more time by last light.

Hymn

Going down
the valley

down
the valley

only a spark
for warmth

among the shadows.
Going to lie down

in darkness
Father

here
and here after.

IV. Nightfishers

I was sinking into a world
whose bars would hold me forever.
— Jonah 2:6

The TVA had a name for it, but everybody around there called it That Dam Town—built for the dam workers. The houses were all small but neat, cedar-shingled. In the middle of the camp was a store and a meeting house.

It was the first place we lived in with electricity. They had lessons at the meeting house where they showed us how to use the cook stove. It took some getting used to.

There were a good many of us in the camp that had been moved off the land but had noplace yet to go. Shortly after we got there, they had a special church meeting one Sunday afternoon for all of us.

I'm not sure what denomination that preacher was, but I believe it was TVA.

He talked about how the land we had left was not a Paradise, not a place of rest, but a place of toil and hardship. Said we had been moved out for a better place to be made, the whole countryside being turned into a land of plenty.

Said we may not know where we would be tomorrow, but to remember that the children of Israel had to go by the wilderness way, too.

Said we ought not to look on ourselves as exiles and strangers, but as a chosen people, just camping outside of Canaan for now, on our way to a promised land.

Lord, forgive me for talking this way about a preacher. But that man was nothing short of a fool. And every word he spoke turned my heart bitter and hard against him.

Nightfishers

The earth wheels on to its dark appointments
no witness
borne to the tiny circle of light
I have raised on black ashes

black stones against the nothingness
I am.
Rising then
I leave my watchfire

make my way down
through pathless river birches
gaunt elders
drawing their shade cloaks around them

as I pass
and come out onto the bank
where night has opened
its empty hand across the lake —

the mirrored stars
only the lights of the summer houses
on Carr's Bluff
only the lights of the nightfishers

drifting on their narrow
doors into the water
where lies my inheritance:
memory of the home I've never seen

half-formed, half-
dissembling shapes
breaking in circles to the surface
sinking back . . .

Some went down to watch them shut the flood gates finally. They put on a big ceremony, with the governor and all.

Others kept going up the ridge every few days to see how the waters were rising.

I never went.

I told them I'd seen floods before. Told them I wanted to see this one even less than any other.

Decoration Day

Places I could never find again
roads I could never retrace . . .
hardtop, gravel, then dirt
deep into Marshall County
one Decoration Day
coming at last
to a cove of black willows along a creek
the ground beyond the trees
turning to water — the lake.

Down through the sweet mint and jewelweed
we helped my grandmother
down to the limestone lip of the bank
where she knelt
unwrapped two loaves of bread she'd made
laid them on the water
two tiny coffins
my father pushing them out into the middle
with a maple switch
my brother and I

following along the bank
watching them drift beyond the shaded mouth
two tiny boats now
sails lowered
riding the current out into the lake
and out of sight
lost in the sunlight sparkling
lost in the gentle waves
like hands reaching.

It's the quiet ones who take things the hardest. We all had shed our share of tears over it, mother and Inez and I, and even your grandfather. But Buell had never said a word about leaving. Not before, not during, or after.

We had already been living in New Covenant about three years. Buell had found work farming for a man over in Calloway County, and him and Cora seemed happy. We would go down and visit them on Sundays about once a month.

Two men dragging for mussels saw him do it. Said they saw him come walking down Cane Fork Road. Or what used to be. Runs right into the lake now.

Said they saw him put down his pole and tackle box. Saw him stoop down, scoop up handfuls of rock, and stuff them into his overall pockets. Saw him walk straight down the road, straight down into the water.

By the time it dawned on them what he was doing, it was too late, they couldn't get to him. He was just gone.

Return

Bright evening stars
come shining.
Night's soothing hand
smoothes the waves along the bank
where oak roots

work their way to the surface
like stitches
fireflies among the sawgrass
like sparks dropping from torches
as I in my borrowed boat

set out.
Leaning into the oars
I picture him
for whom the waters would not part
still lost still wandering

the sunken net of roads below
black flame of his deathlamp
flickering
still searching for landmarks
on his way to take his body home

to lay it down
searching for the faces
that would come to welcome him
calling out hearing only in return
the waves tolling

their mourning bell
as though the living darkness had descended
taking all

stars receding farther into nothing
sun refusing

ever to shine
as though heaven had become all things
above this water
into which I reach my hand now
pull it back

as through a mirror.
The moon at last comes clear,
stone yellow
mote in night's eye,
lays my shadow on the surface

drifting
fellow pilgrim
that never can go down to him
my lantern
the light to which he can never rise.

V. New Covenant Bound

There is a great chasm fixed between us; no one
from our side who wants to reach you can
cross it; and none may pass from your side to ours.
— Luke 16:26–27

Hymn

Going to rise
again

rise again
as stars

begin to fall
like bread from heaven.

Going to take up
my body

children
walk this burning earth

walk it
burning.

We came to New Covenant the same way we left Bethel Grove —
everything we owned tied up on the back of a truck and us still
wondering what kind of a life we were bound for.

Many a family ended up going north. Chicago. Indianapolis.
Detroit. Said those were some sure places to find work at the
time. But all them places were farther away from home than I ever
wanted to be. And I told your grandfather so.

I counted it a blessing, then, when he came in from the camp office
one afternoon and said the County Relief had found him a job of
work in New Covenant.

And none too soon, either. Now that the dam was finished, the
workers' town was to be turned into a tourist camp, and we were to
be turned out, whether we had anyplace to go or not.

The first house we took in New Covenant was a little tar-shingled
shack up on Beechum Hill, back of the quarry.

It felt like a mighty queer thing, sitting up there hearing the street
traffic, seeing the lights spread out over town, and us not knowing a
soul here.

It felt like living in a far country.

Hour of Mercy

Here, again, near the moonwashed pond
where fireflies

rattle their beggar's cups
where a spider's web

raised shining in the canebrake
is a wound in the air

the wind will heal
I bide the dark before sleep.

Hour of mercy and the rose eye
the water I would cross

water that would bear me forth
is a river gone down now into the earth

rising in the veins
of trees channeling out into the air.

Blue hand
of my dying fire

trembles sparks
up into the other side of night

there where the mourning of the lost
goes on

where stars are a dark mansion
a coming and going of torches on a hillside

headlights stringing over Clark Ferry Bridge
entering one by one.

New Covenant wasn't much of a little town then. But it did have two things we were thankful for — the Illinois Central Freight Depot and the Elkhorn Manufacturing Company.

The job they'd found your grandfather was trucking railroad freight around town for T. C. Dillard, the same job he had when he died in 1954. Then I went to work at Elkhorn, sitting at a sewing machine tacking flap pockets on overalls eight and sometimes ten hours a day, which is what I did the next twenty-odd years. Until Mother's mind got so bad I couldn't go off and leave her.

The first time I walked in that factory, I thought I'd either have to suffocate or get out of there. I had never in my life been in such a place. You couldn't get your breath, with all that hammering noise and blue dust hanging in the air. You couldn't see a bit of sunshine — one whole wall was nothing but windows, but they were all sooted and blacked over.

I stuck with it, though. There just wasn't any choice.

But I never missed home so much as when I was in that factory. I'd set my mind wandering back to Bethel Grove. Some days I could picture it so clear, it seemed like it wasn't even me sitting bound to that sewing machine, just my shadow.

I guess the better part of me is still roaming around back there at the home place somewhere. Always will be.

Prayer

There where my breath enters the darkness
and I cannot yet follow

you who are lost
await me

with your signal lanterns your pitchers of milk
on the opposite shore

where you gather thorns
to feed your watchfires

scattered across the snowy fields
where you kneel at the water

washing the clay from your hands.
You who are nothing

nothing but the earth once touched
and made holy

children of dust
once raised to the light —

there you have done my starving for me
there you eat the salt crust

of your longing and are filled.
And what news of my journey

will I bring you in return
what scarred memory

of the last hour
before I cross over to you —

a rain crow lighting on a gate
October wind

harping on the fencewire?
blue dragonfly

the delicate
stained glass webs of its wings

lifting from the footprint
I leave

as I step into my boat?
Until that day

the earth shall free me
and you gather me there to you

beneath the witness tree
to shelter me against the wilderness

you who have suffered the wanderings
of your children

watch over me
here where I seek my comfort

on this stony ground
covering myself with darkness

here
where I wait for the light

to open and receive me
here where I pray —

come down
now to lie near me

to warm yourselves
at my fire.

After all was said and done, the thing I worried about most after we got to New Covenant was keeping the family together.

Your father was the only one of the three I ever feared would leave us. When he was little more than a good-sized boy, he'd walk the mile or so down to the hard road of an evening, just to sit and see if any car lights would pass by. And after we had been in New Covenant a while, he took to sitting by himself down at the station platform, just watching the trains come and go. I was always afraid he had some kind of itch in his feet.

And without the farm, there was just nothing to keep a grown boy occupied. There was surely nothing to keep him in New Covenant, nothing but the movie house and the pool hall. So it wasn't much of a surprise when he came in one morning and said he was going downtown to sign up with the Navy.

It wasn't a surprise, but it was still the second hardest thing I ever did, standing there on the front steps a month later, watching them pull away, him and his brother leaving for Hopkinsville, where he was to catch a train to Nashville and on to Norfolk, Virginia.

I just kept wondering, after everything that had gone on before, what else I would have to give up.

After four years, though, I guess he'd seen as much of the world as he wanted. As soon as the Navy let him go, he came back here, moved right back in.

It wasn't two years before he was married and starting on a family of his own, here in this same house. And he hasn't been much place else since then.

3 Dreams

Digging in the earth
along the alley fence
for things I would need on my journey

a rust blackened
tin spoon
that would feed a fire

a broken cup
to beg with
that would empty itself

shards of colored glass
to piece together on arriving —
a window:

blue angel
after Judgment

planting the white tree
again in the scarlet water . . .

* * *

Grandmother —
I saw you standing in a dooryard in a yellow dress

shading your eyes
a flock of starlings flaring up against the sun

a torn sheet
snapping in the broken window of the house behind you.

*   *   *

A rusted anchor
has been found
on a mountain.

A glove a coin
a length of chain
have washed ashore.

Far out in the night
-colored sea
the great fish

gather
to
name the deserts.

Some people had bought the old Cerulean Springs Hotel and moved the whole thing upstream, out of the way of the lake. After the war, they opened it up again, just like it used to be, hoping to cash in on some of the new tourist trade coming through.

They built up some new baths, there in the spring, like it was years before. There for a while, people were coming from as far away as Louisville and Nashville for a holiday and to take in the waters. It was supposed to be good for whatever ailments you had, to bathe yourself in the spring.

Seems there was this old Holiness preacher lived back up in the woods there, on the other side of the spring. One Sunday afternoon he came down the path to those open-air baths, carrying a Bible and a little wooden crate. People were down in the spring, lounging around on the little stone benches they had set up in the shallow water. Others were laying about on the bank.

Said this old preacher waded out into the spring across from where them people were, set his little crate down, floating there on the water beside him, and started in preaching to them. "*These* are not the waters that heal!" he called out. "Only the living waters of heaven can cure what you're afflicted with!"

Well, them people didn't know quite what to make of it at first, so they just sat and watched him. He just went on preaching.

He told them they were all trespassers and had no business being there. Said that land and that spring wasn't theirs to do with what they wanted. Said they had already defiled the whole countryside with their dam and their lake, and now they were defiling this spring, just like everything else they put their hand to.

Pretty soon, people up at the hotel heard him, and they were gathering out on the yard leading down to the spring. Some of

76

them started to think it was funny, and one of them hollered out, "Amen, brother. Preach it now." Then they all started calling out "Amen" and "Hallelujah" and laughing at the old man.

He just kept on preaching. Said the book of Revelations told about the seven-headed beast that was soon to rise up from the sea and put an end to all their corruption. Said that *then* this land would be put back to the way it was first made to be.

Them people just kept shouting back at the old preacher, laughing at him, calling out their amens and their hallelujahs.

Then the old man stopped and unlatched the lid of that little wooden crate still floating there beside him. He hollered out, "The devil take back the devil's work!" and he reached in and pulled out about four foot of cottonmouth, set it down in the water and watched it shoot out across the spring, straight toward those people sitting there.

Then he reached in and pulled out another one and set it loose. Then another one.

Them people started shooting up out of that water like it was on fire, all hollering and shaking wet and cussing the old man, and even the ones up on the bank started backing back up toward the hotel.

By the time that old preacher let the fifth snake loose, he was the only person anywhere close to that spring.

Said he just picked up his little crate, waded up out of the water, and headed on back up his path into the woods.

I don't imagine any of them people went after him, do you?

Cumberland: Waking after Midnight

Father — the lights along the river no longer call you.
They are only the smoke pots and lanterns

of the black women fishing below Clark Ferry Bridge.
What lies beyond that dark line of trees

no longer summons, *Gather, that none be lost* —
only the night breeze, thornstrung and disputing

in a clutch of wild roses along the bank. Father —
now the blue clouds assemble in their upper room

a few stars scatter among the dust
there where we will soon turn in time with the world.

Now the birth-scarred moon slips free of its cold harbor
and sails on. Coal barges southbound through the channel

the Cumberland pulling her grief along
like a rich purple robe

there where we will soon lean together like old men
our names emptied to be refilled

there where we will soon step out
wearing our morning garments.

c⌒)

We'd been living in New Covenant about a year when a man from the newspaper come by the house. Said he was going around talking to some of the people that had been moved off the river, aiming to write a story about where they ended up and how they were faring.

He asked me what I thought of having electricity now. I allowed that electricity was a wonderful thing, that it made a person's life a good deal easier. Especially a woman's. But I told him I thought I never would get used to an electric cook stove. And I was right. I have yet to get used to it, all these years later.

Then he asked your grandfather something about flood control, about the river finally being brought in line.

Your grandfather spoke right up. Said that if the only way they could make peace with that river was to let it cover as much land as it wanted, then it sounded like the flood was controlling *them*, instead of the other way around.

He asked us if we didn't think people were somewhat better off now, with all the so-called advantages the dam had brought.

I told him there might be *some* people better off, if he meant the land speculators and whoever it was that sold the government all that concrete to build the thing.

But as for myself, I couldn't see how I was better off walking a half mile a day to sit at a sewing machine to help feed us than I would have been out in God's own fresh air raising a garden and helping your grandfather make crops to help feed us.

I told him he could have every bit of it back — electricity included — if I could just go back home, as hard a living as it was at times.

I doubt he wrote that up in his newspaper story, but that's exactly how I felt about it. And I still do.

After everything is gone, you just have to make do with what's left. And that's what we did.

I never came to like the first thing about living in this town. I just got used to it. But after forty-odd years, I've never once called it home.

New Covenant Bound

Now in the last hour
    before the sky tilts
its edge to meet the earth
    the sun to raise
its thorny crown of light
    across the water
I am passing over
    Clark Ferry Bridge
to the opposite shore
    of my dark sojourn
leaving the place of my first birth
    first dust
turning again to face my life
    leaving the dead
to return to theirs
    New Covenant bound.

East again
    the route my elders chose
once named
    The Jefferson Davis Highway
through Cerulean Springs
    a generation gone now
a few streetlamps
    still raising dim haloes
on bent stalks
    a sunken row of Tourist Cabins
leaning through the edge of night
    spear grass and green diamonds
of broken glass
    reclaiming the cracked asphalt
of bait shops and barbecue stands
    the sky bereft of travelers

but a rusting
        cut-tin angel
trumpeting from a pole above a tavern
        called The Tin Angel
beer sign in the window
        flicking
cold blue
        flame of a heart
as I am released again
        to open road
by a billboard sinking into vines
        away behind me
mocking time
        and memory:
a catfish in a sailor's suit
        saying *Welcome*
to Cerulean Springs
        Gate Way to the Great Lakes of the South
— last monument
        to my lost country
and I am rolling into darkness now
        New Covenant bound.

Dropping down into corn and beanflats
        highway bearing with the willows
and water maples
        lining out Soldier Creek
locusts and mudfrogs and weather prophets
        chirring among the nightwood
cold stars
        still hanging on
in their blue heaven.
        Halfway to Caldwell
I cross the L&N
        my landmark —
see it scarring out
        across the Barrens

up into the northern coal fields
       — leave hardtop for the gravel
shortcut into Christian County
       enter the thick crosshatching
of blue pine woods
       skirting the foot of Royer Bluff
then out again into moonlight
       past the reason for the detour:
a scattering of stones
       and crosses
a mute
       white churchhouse
Pilot Rock
       Missionary Baptist
where my name has been enlisted
       some twenty years
falsely now
       for ten
though I would not reclaim it
       would let it lie
as I would ever be
       New Covenant bound.

North for the last leg
       State 106
Pee Dee to Mose Crossing
       farmland rippling into low hills
black dogwoods and redbuds
       brush stroked
on smoked sky
       first lights appearing
in the drifting houses
       kitchen eyes in the dark.
Spring Hill
       and an owl
abandons the ruins of a wellhouse
       south fork of Little River

bleeding moonlight
        down toward Iron Bridge
where Walnut Lane hooks back
        into the caves and low palisades.
Newstead Station
        and the last waysign:
the depot
        still sinking in the corner of a hayfield —
rails of the Cadiz-
        St. Louis Line
two generations gone
        — my own
spent childhood
        sitting on the fallen platform
wondering
        which directions the tracks
once led
        or might have led
then as now
        New Covenant bound.

And off to my left now
        there at last
the burn of gray light
        washed up against
the still-night sky
        above the last line of hills:
aura or ghost
        that draws me on.

I circle wide of town
        coming in from the north
on Buttermilk Pike
        the old drummers' route
climbing Water Tower Hill
        above the empty stockyards

above the gouged
		rock pit of the quarry.

Making the top
		I pull to the side of the road
cut the engine
		lights of New Covenant
spread out below
		constellations
fallen
		indecipherable
like so many the land
		has died for:
the brickyard and seed mills
		loose floors and grain elevators
crumbling down the banks
		the broken shoulder of the river
all given over now
		to Dixonite
King-Phelps Magnetic Wire
		Dodds AmeriGlass
Mid-Continent
		Textile and Clothing
all blazing out the edge of town
		drawing a few headlights
first comers
		for the shift change
sparks
		returning to a flame.

And in the pools of darkness
		scattered through the heart
of Old Town
		I know
the blue dust assembles
		with the leaves and broken glass and trash

in the silenced corners of Elkhorn
    I know the hopper cars
transpire to rust
    along the switchline
back of Armistice Park
    I know the hands of the firehouse clock
mark the same hour
    some thirty-seven years now
as another blackened brick
    unseen
is dropping from the stack of the ice factory
    into the cinder yard.

And I know
    my father
lies waiting.
    I pull back
onto the highway
    start down
to the beginning of my life
    shouldering
its chance
    and forfeit:

one day
    my shadow will rise up
enter me with its burden
    and I will be changed
from this that I am
    into a being of light
one day I'll know
    what I have been
or might have been
    a stranger in a promised land
or only one of the chosen
    roaming

lost in the wilderness
        as only the white moon
rides it out now
        above the lights of home.

I call this moon
        High Lonesome
I call
        this moon
Stone Eye
        black rags of cloud
passing over
        like widows' skirts
and orphans' shirts
        flying —

Credits

Several of these poems appeared previously, sometimes in different form, in the chapbook *Cumberland* (Birmingham, Ala.: Mercy Seat Press, 2007), as well as in the following publications: *Between the Rivers* ("Leaving New Covenant," "Nightfall," "Traveler's Rest," and prose excerpts from "Summons" and "The Crossing"); *Connecticut Review* ("Landscape: Muhlenberg County"); *Georgia Review* ("Homecoming"); *Red Mountain Review* ("Burning Ground"); *Solo* ("Cumberland: Waking after Midnight," "Elders," "Exile," "Twilight," "Waiting for the 12:16"); *Virginia Quarterly Review* ("Eden"); *Wind Magazine* ("Prayer," "There's two ways to ring a church bell . . .").

"Elders" appeared in *What Comes Down to Us: 25 Contemporary Kentucky Poets,* ed. Jeff Worley (Lexington, Ky.: University Press of Kentucky, 2009).

"Hymn" (parts III and V) appeared in *Missing Mountains,* ed. Kristin Johanssen, Bobbie Ann Mason, and Mary Ann Taylor-Hall (Nicholasville, Ky.: Wind Publications, 2005).

The lyrics quoted in "Some people saved up their Briar Rose flour sacks . . ." that begins "Beneath the oak leaves murm'ring lowly" are from "Angel Mary," by A. J. Curtis and J. M. Hubbard (1863).

The lyrics quoted in "Remembrance" are adapted from "Sweet Rose of Heaven," as performed by The Taylor-Griggs Louisiana Melody Makers (Victor Records, 1928).

Index of Titles and First Lines

Titles are shown in *italic* type

About the Author

Tony Crunk is a native of Hopkinsville, Kentucky. His first collection of poetry, *Living in the Resurrection*, was the 1994 selection in the Yale Series of Younger Poets competition. He lives in Birmingham, Alabama.